Write Like A Leader

Jim Kokocki

ISBN: 9798393912604

Imprint: Independently published

Printed in Canada

Foreword from Daniel Rex, Chief Executive Officer Toastmasters International

There are many demands placed on those who serve on Toastmasters International's board of directors, and particularly those in the most senior positions. Toastmaster members expect an International President to effectively chair board meetings, to engage well with our members, and to work well with organizations that host Toastmasters clubs as part of their employee development efforts.

I found it interesting to learn more about Jim's approach to writing his monthly columns. Clearly for any International President advance planning helps in managing this writing task given personal commitments, and the other obligations of volunteer leadership.

Effective writing skills are valuable for all leaders. These skills are even more essential given our continuous use of technology systems to communicate. Good writing helps clarify direction and reduces misunderstandings.

Introduction

International President. That was my title during 2015-2016 when I had the honor to serve in Toastmasters International. Toastmasters is a global organization, a not-for-profit, incorporated in 1924 to empower people to become more effective communicators and leaders. Today, the organization has 15,000 member clubs, and 300,000 actively participating members. Over the years, Toastmasters has empowered millions of eloquent, confident alumni. The organization has prospered, adapted and evolved through wars, recessions, and pandemics.

Serving as International President is a significant leadership role. I suspect if you're reading this book that you're about to embark on a similar leadership assignment. The content in this book pertains to planning elements of communication and engaging broad teams.

Specifically, my purpose is to share how I planned key messages to share with the members of the organization. The most wide-reaching communication vehicle available to me was the recurring monthly columns I, and every President, wrote for the magazine during their term.

Planning these columns in advance enabled me to clarify my thinking, eased the task of writing, and the planned content inspired my speeches and videos that were shared with various groups of the membership.

Planning and writing on these topics improved my speaking. Speaking on these topics improved my writing. I hope you find this content helpful with your planning, speaking, and writing.

The Role of International President

2024 will serve as Toastmaster's 100th anniversary. That's an amazing achievement for any organization. The founder, Dr. Ralph Smedley, started the organization because he was working with the YMCAs back in the day and observed that the young men needed an environment where they could work on their communication and leadership skills. He would never have imagined the global impact and reach that the organization has attained.

Every International President has significant responsibility to the members and the organization. One responsibility is to write a monthly column for the magazine The

Toastmaster. The President's monthly column is titled Viewpoint and the content is the choice of the President.

There are three key functions to the role of International President. First, to serve as an internal ambassador with the clubs and members. Second, to serve as an external ambassador with companies who have one or more Toastmaster clubs, or desire so, within their organization as part of their development program for employees. And third, to serve as the Chair of the Board of Directors.

In preparation for my twelve months at the helm, I made notes months in advance about topics I might write about. These were topics that I believed were important for the readers and the organization, and they were topics for which I had some passion.

I had an opportunity each month to connect with members and share these topics. I wanted to recognize their progress and achievement, to emphasize the immense benefits of the simple communication tasks Toastmasters members perform regularly at meetings, and to encourage members and leaders to pursue opportunities for improvement within their clubs. No matter how successful, every organization has opportunity for improvement.

As a leader and communicator, I recognize some people process information best by reading, some by listening, some by watching video, and of course everyone learns by participating in experiential learning. Toastmaster clubs provide exceptional experiential learning opportunities to those who embrace opportunity.

During my year as President, I had the chance to meet and speak with thousands of Toastmasters members, to provide commentary via video, and to use the written word in the monthly column and in other publications.

In this book I will share the strategy and intention behind each column. Speeches need to have purpose, and columns and other written material need to have purpose. For each monthly column, I'll describe the intention, share the column that was published, and comment on any results that were obvious. My hope Is that this is helpful for anyone who takes on a leadership role in any organization, and has the opportunity to connect similarly with a column.

Should you be interested in other Viewpoint columns, please visit:

https://www.toastmasters.org/Magazine/listing/category/Viewpoint

The catalog of magazines is available here https://www.toastmasters.org/magazine/issues

My Initial Planning in 2015

First, a couple of questions for you. Where do you see your organization in five years? How has it progressed, and what were some of the changes in people's behaviors that enabled this progress?

As I prepared for my role, I considered how I believed the organization could evolve and how the actions of our thousands of volunteer leaders would shape such an evolution. Toastmasters is primarily a network of Toastmaster clubs around the world, and my focus was on the individual members and the clubs, where the members engage to practice and refine their communication and leadership skills. I had no direct control of the behaviors in any of the 15,000 member clubs, my only power was to inspire behavior of club members in a manner that I thought would be helpful to the long-term success of our clubs, for the benefit of all club members.

Before my term began, staff responsible for the magazine asked me if there were topics I planned to write about, as that would assist them in planning monthly themes for the magazine. That was easy. I had been developing a list for months. I let them know that my prevailing themes would be around driving more awareness and knowledge of each club and of Toastmasters in general, keeping local leaders focused on helping clubs prosper and meeting assigned goals, and being proud of their successes but not complacent.

I indicated that additionally I hoped to help members realize how the skills they practice in our clubs are transferable to their community, family and business lives. These leadership skills include focusing on specific issues and not quirky personalities, and on protecting the self-esteem of colleagues, as well as listening, speaking, organizing among others.

Appendix A contains my email response to this request from magazine staff.

September 2015 Strategy - Focus on Public Relations

My first column was titled <u>What Do Prospective Members Want To Know?</u> Now I find that phrasing a little awkward. My intention was to encourage club leaders to boost their public relations activity by simply sharing images of their meetings. Images of members at meetings laughing, speaking, and enjoying themselves convey information about the supportive and friendly environment. These days images and video content dominate social media, but it was less so in 2015. There was opportunity in 2015, and there remains so today.

There was a humorous incident resulting from this column. In 2015 we mailed paper copies of the magazine to every member in the world, although currently distribution is entirely online. Distribution was performed with a series of ten mail cycles each month, so there was variability in when members would receive their copy of the magazine. In this September column I wrote about the need to drive public awareness when marketing any product or service. If customers aren't aware a product exists, they're obviously not going to buy the product, and therefore, marketers need to boost awareness and knowledge.

To illustrate the need for awareness, and the power of awareness, I mentioned that my friend and future International President Balraj Arunasalam had made me aware of a simple, effective travel product called packing cubes, which are particularly helpful for long trips with several stops. Packing cubes are a simple product that enable travelers to organize clothes and content by category so luggage isn't a huge mish-mash. Balraj had told me how he used packing cubes for long trips, and I had become an enthusiastic packing cube customer once I became aware of the benefit.

This was an excellent example of driving awareness of a helpful product, and enabling my subsequent purchase, so I wrote about this example in the column. I had not been aware of packing cubes, Balraj made me aware, and as a result I was an enthusiastic customer. I had moved quickly through the buying cycle.

I had neglected to tell Balraj that I was going to mention him in the column. Then, towards the end of September, after the magazine made its way around the world, I was talking with Balraj and he mentioned that he received his copy of the magazine in late September and it solved a mystery for him. He said he had been receiving email from members all around the world asking him about packing cubes and he didn't know why. I apologized and told him I should have let him know I was mentioning him in that first column.

Did the column improve results and club public relations efforts? It's difficult to assess. But Balraj's experience indicates to me that members did read the column. If more members learned about packing cubes, then I expect some were influenced to use more images in the promotion of their Toastmaster club. All organizations, including Toastmaster clubs, need to consistently drive awareness and knowledge for prospective members and customers.

Here is that September 2015 column.

What Do Prospective Members Want To Know?

What questions did you have in mind before you walked into your first Toastmasters meeting?

You likely had questions such as these. Do people dress casually or in business attire? Are there people my age? Are there men and women? Is it ethnically diverse? Is the environment quite serious and formal or do people have a little bit of fun?

Pictures from your club meetings can answer most of these questions for prospective members. I occasionally search

Twitter, Instagram and Facebook for Toastmasters and I enjoy seeing pictures from your club meetings. In your casual photos I often see your members speaking, your room setup, your agendas, and often your preferences in coffee brands and soft drinks. Do you agree with the old saying that a picture is worth a thousand words?

I hope your club is using available tools to promote images of your club to the world. Marketing and sales models tell us that if people are not aware that you exist, they won't buy your service. And if people are aware you exist but lack knowledge of what you do, they won't buy your service. But when people have awareness and knowledge, interest can grow, desire to purchase can grow, and more people will take action to purchase. You can probably think of a product or service that you eagerly purchased once you had awareness and knowledge. First Vice-President Balraj Arunasalam, DTM recently told me about a packing cube product for travelers that I wish I had known about ten years ago.

Applying the marketing model to your club, it becomes apparent that we can use photos to drive awareness and knowledge for prospective members. Still today, too many people say they have never heard of Toastmasters, or they have heard of us but they don't have any idea what we do. I'm sure you have heard your friends and co-workers make such statements. Images of your members speaking and having fun at your meetings can help immensely in driving awareness and knowledge of your club, and of Toastmasters in general.

Thank you for your membership in Toastmasters. I'm sure you are enjoying benefits far beyond what you initially expected. Let's find methods to reach more people so that they, like us, can realize benefits from participating in one of our supportive clubs.

October 2015 Strategy – Leaders Achieve Goals

In my October column my strategy was to get club leaders focused on achieving their assigned goals. Leadership is about setting goals, or having goals assigned, and then working to achieve them. In general, leaders in any organization, whether for-profit or not-for-profit, need to prioritize and focus time, energy, money and other resources to reach results.

Sometimes leaders can choose their own goals, but for most leaders, higher-level managers or a board of directors, assign goals. Effective leaders achieve these goals quite consistently. Every Toastmasters club in the world is asked to work towards ten assigned goals and become a Distinguished Club, which means reaching at least five of their ten assigned goals by July 1st.

Any International President wants every member to achieve his or her personal communication and leadership goals. In my opinion, that's most likely to occur in a club where the leaders are focused on reaching assigned objectives.

With this column I wanted to reinforce the developmental opportunity available to all volunteer leaders in Toastmasters. That leadership opportunity is to learn to direct energy and resources to achieving their assigned goals.

Did this result in a cohort of leaders eager to achieve results in any of their future endeavors? It's difficult to say, however, our results dashboards indicate that in 2015-2016 54.4% of clubs (8,695 of 15,977) achieved at least the minimum targets to achieve Distinguished, or higher.

Distinguished
Club Results

	2014-15	**2015-16**	**2016-17**
Distinguished Clubs	8,296	8,695	8,521
Total Clubs	15,406	15,977	16,469
Percent achieving Distinguished +	53.8%	54.4%	51.7%

Here is that October column.

October 2015 Viewpoint

Personal Development Tucked Into Real Work – Achieving Results

What would you say that leaders do?

There are many ways to answer the question. They inspire, they coach, they support, they delegate when appropriate, and so on. In the broader world the most in demand leaders consistently achieve results. In return they receive increasingly demanding assignments.

I recognize that not everybody is looking for increasingly demanding assignments, but it's nice to be in a position where they're made available because of one's past successes.

Sometimes in organizations important and urgent work has to be done so the strongest performers are assigned to complete it. In this case little personal development takes place. Conversely, sometimes in organizations training takes place without a clear view of how it fits with an employee's plan for personal development. However, the most fulfilling personal development happens when people have challenging tasks and important work needs to be completed.

That's part of the brilliance of the Toastmasters leadership program. We tuck personal development into real work, for example becoming a Distinguished Club.

For club leaders, this is our organization's standard of achievement - to become a Distinguished Club. If you are a club leader, I encourage you to regularly provide status updates and inform your members about club goals and progress, and to recognize behaviors that will lead to club achievement. If you're not in a formal club leadership role, please ask your club leaders how you can contribute to club achievement while you work on your personal development with us. For example, all of our members can help their clubs become distinguished by inviting new members or completing an educational award.

Often, it's difficult for us to recognize our own personal growth. But people around us notice our personal growth much more easily. In our everyday lives our Toastmasters members display our improved communication skills, interpersonal relations, support for our team members, and an ability to find ways to contribute to team and organizational achievement.

If you're interested in reading more on this topic, I recommend an article titled Leadership That Gets Results in Harvard Business Review. This is very accessible online.

Toastmasters exists to serve our members. I'm interested to see members develop transferrable skills that help them in their personal and professional lives. It is my sincere desire that every member achieves his or her personal goals within Toastmasters while developing the ability to help their club achieve results.

November 2015 – Strategy – Recognize Your Leadership Development

In 2015 the organization was in the early stages of updating our educational program and platform. Back then the model was paper based with a series of project manuals, and the "Revised Educational Program," which would soon be known as Pathways, would be primarily online, with an option to print at an additional cost to the member.

Every iteration of our educational program over the years has served the organization well. In 2015, when a member joined, we would mail from California two manuals of developmental projects. They'd arrive quite speedily to new members in North America, but less so in many of the 145 countries where we have active members, where it might take weeks to arrive. In some of those countries, passionate, committed local Toastmaster leaders maintained a stockpile of manuals in order to quickly enable a new member to start participating.

When a guest sees our experiential learning environment, and is excited to join, we want to quickly enable them to prepare a first speech and begin their developmental journey with us. Pathways promised, and delivered, immediate access to material once the member was activated. Pathways development and implementation was a difficult and slow project for the organization, and met with some resistance, which is inherent with any change. However, enabling members anywhere in the world to quickly access the educational material with a decent internet connection, has been a tremendous investment for meeting the needs of current and future members.

In this column, I referenced the development of the Revised Educational Program, however the larger message was intended to help members realize how seemingly simple functions they perform at any Toastmasters meeting exercised and developed their leadership skills.

In the column, I mention counting "ums and ahs." This is a practice at most Toastmaster meetings. A member is assigned the role of noting the quantity and style of distracting non-words attendees use in their verbal communication, and then share that at the end of the meeting with grace and empathy. These non-words, or filler words, typically escape as 'ums and ahs." Effective speakers use a minimum of filler words. Few will entirely eliminate their use, but effective speakers will reduce them so their listeners do not have to work to filter these as they listen and consider a message. Audiences shouldn't need to work hard to comprehend a message.

Did the column result in members better recognizing the transferable skills practiced as they perform simple functions at their club meetings? It is difficult to assess, however it seems that terms such as "transferable skills" are more prevalent in our material these days. I'll choose to believe I had some influence on this.

Here is the November column.

Viewpoint – November 2015

Practicing Leadership Skills at Every Meeting

Back in 2011 when we launched the tag line "Where Leaders Are Made,' I thought we may have been ahead of ourselves. In my view, while we have been quite strong at developing leaders, we had not formalized the skills, competencies and the educational development approach. These days when I see our progress reports on our Revised Educational Program (REP), I feel very confident that our REP will address these gaps. So good for us for setting our expectations high.

Now, soon after we introduced the "Where Leaders Are Made" tagline I read something and it caused me to change my opinion. What I read provided another perspective on how we are so very strong at developing leaders.

A leadership consultant wrote about his work consulting, advising and developing leaders in major organizations. He described a very special assignment ---- an assignment in which he was asked to teach leadership to 3rd and 4th grade school kids.

He wrote that the kids just got it – they understood leadership easily. But he wrote that with 3rd and 4th graders leadership skills aren't about writing mission statements and dealing with poor performers. For this age leadership is about focusing on the problem and not the person or personality, and about protecting the self-esteem of their colleagues.

Focusing on the problem and not the person. Protecting the self-esteem of colleagues. Are those leadership skills?

I believe these are leadership skills for any age. And they're leadership skills that could be more widely deployed in our world today. And they are leadership skills you practice at every Toastmasters meeting.

When a new member presents an Icebreaker speech and feels as if he has beaten the world, as he raced through a four-to-six minute speech in three minutes flat with 30 ums and ahs, I know you protect his self-esteem. You've seen this in your club. I remember this because it is quite close to the Icebreaker I delivered back in 1987.

When you evaluate a speech that expresses a point of view you don't personally agree with, I'm confident you offer feedback on whether the speaker achieved her objectives, despite your differing point of view.

Focusing on the problem, not the person. Protecting the self-esteem of colleagues. These are real world leadership skills that help you regardless of your formal position in your organization or community.

I ask each of you as leaders, regardless of your formal positions, to create and support an environment in which we focus on the objectives or problems – and provide positive support to our team members, as we work together to accomplish our club goals in adherence to our core values of integrity, respect, excellence, and service.

December 2015 Strategy– Find Chances to Mentor

Many organizations struggle with onboarding and developing new employees, or members. Mentorship is immensely helpful in these areas. While mentorship is much written about and talked about, I believe many organizations struggle to enable or implement effective mentorship models.

My strategy with this column was to encourage members to reflect on their mentorship experiences and then talk about them, preferably in speeches at their club meetings. Often when someone first visits a Toastmasters club, they observe the talent in the room and sometimes the newcomer believes she won't ever reach such a level of performance. That's not an accurate assessment because our members become confident and capable as a result of their participation. When members talk about their journeys, and the challenges they had initially, and then how some advice from a mentor aided their development, new members can understand other developmental journeys and the gains available when participating meaningfully.

In the column I shared my experience in joining the organization, and the guidance from my first two mentors Bill and Arnold during our pre-meeting sessions over snacks and drinks.

My strategy was to facilitate more dialogue about mentoring, and more mentoring engagements for the benefit of prospective protegees and the mentors themselves. Was the strategy successful? Again, this is difficult to assess, although I did receive several comments about what I wrote about my experience with Arnold and Bill. At a minimum there was some readership.

Here is that December column.

December 2015 Viewpoint

What Does Mentorship Look Like?

I'm always interested to hear how our members joined Toastmasters. Many people delayed the decision for a long time. Some of the more adventurous amongst us were invited to attend having no idea what to expect at a meeting and we attended anyway.

I joined back in 1987 because two co-workers, Arnold and Bill, came to my desk and said "you're a pretty smart guy Jim but you say nothing at meetings. Come with us to a Saint John Toastmasters meeting."

It was a good fit. I was strong technically as a COBOL programmer but was loath to speak up. The club met from 6pm-8pm on Mondays. It still does. But back then we met in a conference room at a mid-tier hotel. Arnold, Bill and I would each leave the office around 5pm and meet in the small bar at the hotel. The beauty of this was we had access to the luncheon salads that sat on ice all day with the purchase of just one beverage. Sometimes I'd have a soft drink. And we'd dine on the macaroni salad, the three-bean salad, and every week there was a salad made of three kinds of cold cuts. I wouldn't indulge in this gastrointestinal experiment today, but back then it seemed to make sense.

My point in telling this story is that every I week I was able to spend about 45 minutes with my first two mentors in Toastmasters. I remember nervously rehearsing my 30 second duty description with them the first occasion when I was scheduled to serve as Timer.

Does your club facilitate mentoring relationships? Are you perceived as personally accessible to mentor new members? It's a busy world we live in and sometimes our actions send a different message than our intentions.

If I had had a difficult entry to Toastmasters, perhaps I wouldn't be in this position to offer this column. Mentoring is so important to the member experience, and member experience is one of the three pillars of the Toastmasters strategic plan. Every member can make a direct contribution to achieving the three pillars, for example by improving the experience for one member by serving as a mentor.

As we develop our needs from mentors evolve. The final phase of these relationships sees the two people close their mentoring relationship and redefine the relationship. Please speak at your club about some of your mentoring relationships. Talk about your needs at the time and how you evolved. Sharing your stories will help us make progress on the three pillars of our Toastmasters strategic plan.

January 2016 Strategy – Talk with People, Email Isn't Enough

My strategy with this column was to encourage more phone calls and face-to-face communication and less reliance on email and other electronic messaging. Now there are more vehicles for direct communication like Zoom and Skype, and collectively, we still don't use them enough.

We continue to rely too much on email in trying to connect with people. It's easy to send an email isn't it? I observed, and continue to observe, this over reliance. Sometimes in an office, two employees in near proximity will email back and forth when a short walk and conversation would be faster and would likely lead to a better result for both parties.

The volume of e-messaging has only increased. We still have many more opportunities to talk rather than rely on electronic messaging. I continue to find person-to-person communication most effective to manage any task that has some complexity. Email is convenient, but lacks nuance. It is also easier for people to ignore or become lost in volume.

Was my strategy successful?

No.

January 2016 Viewpoint

Leadership and email

Some years ago, I was working in the mobile phone business when text messaging was just becoming popular. Sometimes friends would come to me and say with considerable passion "Jim you need to help me with my son's huge text messaging charges. The worst of the issue is that most of the time he's texting his girlfriend who's on the sofa right next to him!" Crazy, isn't it?

But still today I think we often get the mix between messaging and talking incorrect. It is difficult, and maybe impossible, to understand the emotional content of a response in an email. It can be difficult enough when you're sitting across from another person. However, when you are sitting across from someone you do get clues from the tone of voice, facial expression, eye contact, speed of response, among other subtleties.

Our various communities of interest need more live conversations to occur. In Toastmasters, I also believe our club members need to have more live conversations whether that takes place on the phone or face-to-face.

When a new member who is preparing his Icebreaker emails that he's not ready to deliver his speech, in what way is he not ready? Is it that he hasn't prepared his text or outline, or he's feeling too nervous to begin his Toastmasters journey. When a member who has been developing well, emails that she can't serve as Toastmaster, in what way is she not ready? Is it a matter of content, or other commitments, or nervousness that a mentoring conversation can help overcome?

If you're a club leader, or the Toastmaster who must confirm duty holder assignments, I ask you to not rely solely on email. Direct communication is much more effective in asking questions and clarifying, and in coaching and mentoring one another. Whether you're in a formal club leadership position or not, you have opportunity to exercise these leadership skills. And these are leadership skills that will help you in other areas of your life.

The purpose of my column isn't to dismiss the effectiveness of email. It's very effective to communicate results, progress and assignments. It's terrible for communicating sentiment and for coaching, mentoring, and developing those around us. I hope as you explore the fullness of your opportunities in your Toastmaster club that you are taking the time to speak with other members, and to coach, mentor, and develop those around you. You'll benefit and your club will become stronger.

February 2016 – Strategy

This column was intended to promote one of our annual membership campaigns.

Every year Toastmasters runs three membership programs to encourage club leaders to take action and attract new members. Each program lasts for two months, therefore for six months of the year, Toastmasters operates campaigns encouraging clubs to invite guests and perform some public relations work. In February and March, the campaign is called Talk Up Toastmasters. I wrote the February 2016 column to drive further awareness of Talk

Up Toastmasters with club leaders, and all club members. Toastmasters staff in Colorado manage everything about the programs from promotional material, measurement, reward and recognition. Local club leaders need only focus on attracting guests who may become members.

Some clubs are very good at promotion, at inviting guests, and attracting new members. Some clubs neglect these functions and membership dwindles. A club may offer a stellar, supportive developmental environment, however without some promotion, it is unlikely to attract new members.

Part of a management function is to attract new customers, or new members, because some will lapse. In Toastmaster clubs, over time, a member will achieve her personal goals and move on to other developmental opportunities. Some, like me, will stay with Toastmasters to continue to regularly exercise communication and leadership skills within one of our clubs, but others will exercise these skills elsewhere, perhaps in another not-for-profit addressing other community needs.

Many others take on additional work responsibilities and job promotions as a result of the improved communication and leadership abilities they now exhibit as a result of their Toastmasters participation. Some get new jobs and move to new towns and cities. Members move on, and clubs need to attract guests and new members. This is a direct result of the club successfully empowering skill development for their members.

As a management function, club leaders need to continue to promote the club and invite guests.

Did my column drive improved results. No. The campaign results in 2015-2016 were similar results in the prior and next year.

	Talk Up Toastmasters		
	2014-15	**2015-16**	**2016-17**
End of January new member count	77,565	80,885	80,026
End of March new member count	100,937	106,701	105,689
Change	23,372	25,816	25,663
Percent change	23.2%	24.2%	24.3%

If you're interested to delve further into the data, please visit

https://dashboards.toastmasters.org/2015-2016/?id=55&month=3

Here is the February column.

February 2016 – Talk Up Toastmasters

The number of people I meet who are not aware of Toastmasters, or who don't have knowledge of what we do, surprises me. Guided by the organization's strategic plan, this month the Board of Directors considered approaches to increase the overall awareness of, and participation in, Toastmasters. As a nonprofit, we will focus significantly on tools and techniques that can be used by local clubs and district leaders. The ultimate result of increased awareness will be greater membership in our existing and new clubs.

One existing program to help with awareness and participation is Talk Up Toastmasters, a membership-building campaign for clubs that run in February and March each year. I encourage every club to participate. Campaigns like this remind us to promote our clubs, bring guests to club meetings and invite them to join and develop their skills in our supportive environment.

Toastmasters International surveys samples of members who do not renew their membership. (To find the survey report, go to http://bit.ly/1MwpLwm.) In the survey, non-renewing members say the likelihood they would recommend Toastmasters to a friend, family member or colleague is 8.1 on a scale of 0 to 10. In addition, 77.3 percent of non-renewing members report that they intend to renew soon or may renew in the future. Quite good.

As to the reasons for not renewing their membership, 13 percent cite the meeting time or location of their club, and close to five percent mention the member attendance. If only we could direct these past members to other clubs where their needs found a better match.

I ask you to promote Talk Up Toastmasters in your club. It's a great speech topic in itself. I recall speaking on this once and a newer member said afterwards, "I didn't know we were looking for new members," and the next week she brought two guests. Sometimes we can mistakenly assume that newer members fully see and understand how our clubs operate.

Have some fun as you promote Talk Up Toastmasters. Remind people that any club that adds five new, dual or reinstated members with a join date between February 1 and March 31 will receive a special **Talk Up Toastmasters** ribbon to display on their club's banner. You can learn more by signing in to www.toastmasters.org/MembershipPrograms and then clicking on **Membership Building Programs for Clubs** in the Helpful Resources section.

In addition, when individual Toastmasters sponsor five, 10 or 15 new members in a program year (July 1 to June 30), they will receive special prizes. Learn more by signing in to the same page mentioned above and clicking on **Membership Building Program for Individuals**.

Toastmasters has been very successful over our 91 years thanks to the achievements and performance of our members, the work of our volunteer leaders and our strong culture. We have the capacity to enable many more people to develop their skills. Increased awareness, and membership-building campaigns, can help us do just that.

March 2016 Strategy

This column was a late change to my plan. It was inspired because of something I posted on social media. Each year members achieve educational levels and awards. Once completed a certificate is available and is signed by the

International President and CEO. In 2016 we automatically mailed these certificates to award recipients.

In early 2016, while I served as International President, I completed one of these levels and received a certificate in the mail celebrating my achievement, with the signature of CEO Daniel Rex and the International President. I was the International President. I saw some humor in that and posted a photo of the certificate. The post received hundreds of likes and comments.

This column was a chance to remind the members worldwide, that I was, and am, a member of a local club and I continue to work in our world-class educational program, and to exercise my communication and leadership muscles. All members need to exercise their skills, and deliver speeches. When that takes place, members continue to receive recognition for completions.

The column also acknowledges some of the dynamic of board work, in recapping some mild disagreement back in the day about formalizing a program with a series of speeches, thereby providing a path to "completion'" which our founder Ralph Smedley correctly saw as a bit of a trap. Still. to some extent today I hear Toastmaster members indicate they've completed all the educational material and there's nothing new for them to work on. However, the essence of public speaking is to identify a topic, craft a speech, deliver it to an audience, and evaluate how well it was received and interpreted. While path and level completion is embedded in the program, it is the regular practice of communication skills that results in improvement.

Here is the March column.

Recently I was reading through my copy of <u>The Story of Toastmasters,</u> Volume 1. Some years ago I highlighted a passage in which our founder, Ralph C. Smedley, wrote about introducing the Basic Training for Toastmasters manual in 1942. The organization was founded in 1924, and the Manual of Instructions for clubs came out in 1928—but there was no in-depth instruction about public speaking until the Basic Training manual came out 14 years later.

Smedley was a brilliant man, and he was not in favor of creating a formal "course" or even providing recognition for completing the 12 projects in Basic Training. Such recognition, he wrote, could be viewed by some members as a "graduation diploma," and he considered that a mistake, since he was in favor of lifelong learning.

Despite Smedley's concerns, Toastmasters awarded the first Certificate of Merit in June 1946. Smedley was leery of the graduation concept because he recognized that speaking and leadership are skills, and skills require regular practice. In my conversations with people about Toastmasters, I say that to be an effective leader or speaker you need three elements: a base of knowledge, regular practice and feedback on performance. All of these elements are available in our worldwide network of clubs. To be good at anything requires not only regular practice— but practicing the right things. Athletes regularly practice basic skills to keep sharp. Legendary basketball player Michael Jordan once said, "You can practice shooting eight hours a day, but if your technique is wrong, then all you become is very good at shooting the wrong way. Get the fundamentals down and the level of everything you do will rise."

This past October, I received another Competent Communicator award. I posted a picture of the certificate on Facebook because the award was presented to member James B. Kokocki and awarded by International President Jim Kokocki. Isn't that cool? I was surprised by some of the posted comments: Many of you were surprised to learn that I continue to deliver speeches from the manuals. I do continue to work through the projects and practice the basic skills. And I still find opportunity for improvement. For example, I now prefer to speak without a lectern, but I learned, from a recent presentation where I had a significant number of items to cover, that sometimes it is better to be near, or behind, the lectern. Ralph Smedley was a brilliant man. He recognized that maintaining skills requires regular practice. I sincerely hope that you continue to enjoy your membership and the opportunities to practice your speaking and leadership skills in your supportive club.

April 2016 – Strategy

Serving as International President enabled me to connect with members around the world, often face-to-face. I was, and remain, fascinated how our structured meeting format and educational programs empower individuals in diverse countries and regions, despite differing political, social, economic, and technological environments. My intention with this column was to help members realize the breadth of our organization in which people all over the world develop their skills.

Every member joins one of our Toastmaster clubs. Sometimes, they join more than one club, but typically they join one and begin a developmental journey. In the club they exercise public speaking and other communication skills. They also use and practice leadership skills and various soft skills. Millions of people have benefitted from spending some time as a member of a Toastmasters club.

There was a funny occurrence while developing this column. As per our practice, I would write a column and when I thought it was 95% ready for publication, I'd send it to the editors. Our staff editors would then edit for consistency in voice, and for errors or improvement of course. In this column, I planted a very funny joke about the Toronto Maple Leafs, a National Hockey League team.

I live in the Canadian city of Saint John, which is about 1,500 kilometers east of Toronto.

When our editors sent me their proposed edited version of this column, prior to publication, they had removed my very funny joke. When I saw that my joke was removed, I talked with Paul, one of the editors. I asked why my joke was removed. He thought it might upset some people in Toronto, which was a valid concern. I explained that people in Toronto know their hockey team is bad, and joke about it themselves. Besides, the column was to be published in April, and the Maple Leafs season would be over. In the end, my very funny joke was published. While Paul was correct that some might have found it upsetting, I only received positive comments about my acknowledgement of their perennially bad professional hockey team. As I write this, the Toronto Maple Leafs are actually a pretty good team – finally.

April 2016 – Viewpoint

Empowering Members Worldwide

One of the joys of my position as International President is connecting with members around the world. I'm struck by our common mission, and our common goals and ambitions, despite our vastly different personal circumstances. I consistently see members focused on goal achievement and skill development, and club leaders focused on providing excellent, supportive environments where their members can develop and achieve. In October (2015), I traveled to District 74 in southern Africa, where I visited South Africa and Zimbabwe in my role as an ambassador for the organization. South Africa has 11 official languages, including Xhosa, the language of the ethnic group to which Nelson Mandela belonged. At the district conference, I attended a speaker showcase where several Toastmasters used their skills to deliver speeches in Xhosa. This was memorable for many reasons, not the least of which is that Xhosa contains nearly 20 different clicking sounds as a component of the language.

Then in November, I visited District 60 in Toronto, a vibrant, multicultural city with a perennially bad professional hockey team. One of the district's major initiatives is a focus on the Toastmasters Youth Leadership Program (YLP). I attended a ceremony with local mayors and councilors for a group of YLP graduates and left impressed with the skills of these young people and the commitment of Toastmasters who invest time and energy to help such individuals develop. Later I visited District 95 in Central, Eastern and Northern Europe. This district is composed of 17 countries and more than 230 clubs. Four-hundred members traveled significant distances to enjoy the district conference in Prague. Some members came from Russia; currently we only have a handful of clubs in that country, but we have the potential to empower many people there. I'm confident the talented young leaders I met at the conference will pursue club growth opportunities as well as their own personal development as they work to expand Toastmasters membership throughout the region.

It is a tremendous honor to serve as International President. From time to time, I read the writings of Dr. Ralph Smedley, our organization's founder. Here are a couple of passages he wrote in 1959. (Please keep in mind that, at the time, Toastmasters membership included only men.)

"While our language and our customs have changed, men differ very little in fundamentals from the men of half a century ago. They have similar ambitions, difficulties, and impediments to progress. While conditions have changed, human nature and human needs have not been greatly altered."

Smedley was strongly focused on the individual. What are some of the joys you've experienced as a Toastmaster?

May 2016 – Strategy

In this column my intention was to acknowledge the pride members have in their clubs, and encourage them to focus on their assigned club goals.

We continue to celebrate our clubs and members, and to inspire our local club leaders to achieve club goals. Club leaders develop best, in my opinion, when they focus on meeting their assigned goals and finishing the year as one of our Distinguished Clubs. This column was also a chance to remind members of our proud history. The founder of Toastmasters is Dr. Ralph Smedley. Were he beginning his ambitious task today, we'd call him a social entrepreneur and he would be widely celebrated.

The book The Story of Toastmasters describes how Smedley saw the need for young men to develop communication and leadership skills, and how he crafted a supportive, repeatable environment to develop Toastmasters clubs all over the United States. He began in 1903 and the organization was finally incorporated in 1924. The man was persistent, and a visionary.

We currently have over 15,000 clubs led by an ever-changing group of local leaders who developed in their clubs, and have become advocates and exemplars of the organization. It's important that our members be proud of their clubs and Toastmasters International. Proud but not complacent.

May 2016 – Viewpoint

The Best Club in the World

It seems that every member I speak with believes he or she belongs to the best Toastmasters club in the world. As International President, this gives me great comfort. I'm delighted with the pride each of you has in your club. I'm delighted too, to hear about the plans and efforts of our club leaders around the world to provide quality club environments that enable member achievement. The club is where each member is introduced to Toastmasters and regularly practices communication and leadership skills.

Sometimes members suggest to me that we should consider changing the term club to chapter or something more business-oriented. Personally, I would never be in favor of that. Club is part of our history and part of our compelling story. Isn't it amazing that one man back in 1903 saw a need to train individuals in communication and leadership skills and took the action that ultimately led to the 1924 birth of the Toastmasters organization. That man, Ralph Smedley, later wrote about the early deliberations that led to calling our assemblies clubs. As educational director of the YMCA in Bloomington, Illinois, he worked with his team on an appropriate term for this group he envisioned. They considered public speaking class, debating society and literary society before settling on The Toastmasters Club.

The name "offers a suggestion of a pleasant, social atmosphere, free from anything like work or study," wrote Smedley. This fits well with our longtime emphasis on the supportive environment of our clubs.

As we enter the final few months of our Toastmasters year, I hope your club is on track to achieve its goal of Distinguished status or better. This is also the time of district conferences. I hope you choose to attend your district conference and take the opportunity to share your time and experiences with fellow members there.

Toastmasters are optimistic, enthusiastic people working on their personal development and taking an interest in the self-development of those around them. You are the kind of people I like to be around!

A Toastmasters club is the best club in the world. We share a mission to empower individuals to become more effective communicators and leaders. Our story is compelling. Smedley's story is compelling. I hope when you meet other Toastmasters at your district conference, you share stories about why you are convinced that your club is the best in the world.

June 2016 Strategy

Our Toastmasters year operates from July 1st until June 30th. As we approach year-end, committed leaders work to achieve year end targets. The most successful consistently reach their annual targets.

Rarely, but sometimes, leaders become overly creative in their methods to reach year-end targets, and some stretch the rules. I hope every club, and every team, has the experience of realizing achievement. As year-end nears, many leaders put renewed energy into achieving year-end targets, and our staff manage a great deal of volume with new member applications and completion levels in our educational program, two of our key measures of results.

At year-end there is a large volume of activity with our 15,000 clubs. Staff processing these applications and awards sometimes notice unusual activity, and perform periodic spot checks that can offer explanations for irregular results, which are often valid. For example, it sometimes happens that club leaders don't process educational achievements as they occur during the year, and then rush to process them as year-end approaches. That said, there have been instances where no reasonable explanation exists. Sometimes a phone call uncovers creative methods to artificially attain year-end targets.

The purpose of this column was to remind leaders of our core values of integrity, service, respect and excellence. Still, almost ten years since this column was published, I will receive a few emails during the year from members who were searching for material around core values and they find this column online. When I wrote it, I thought it was simplistic, but easily relatable. It seems to endure.

It was worthwhile to remind members of our core values. Note that "table topics," referenced in the column, are our regular round of off-the-cuff speaking exercises performed at club meetings.

June 2016 Viewpoint

Toastmasters Core Values

Which is more important: integrity, respect, service or excellence?

Sometimes members ask which of our organization's four core values is most important. Of course, none take precedence over the others. Each one is equally important for members and all leaders.

A discussion around core values can make for a very good round of Table Topics in your club. Our core values align closely with those of other organizations, and questions related to these and similar values sometimes come up during job interviews. I'll offer some thoughts on these four values.

What does **integrity** mean in our clubs? For every member, integrity means living up to the Toastmasters promise. That promise includes attending club meetings regularly, preparing for meeting assignments, helping maintain a positive environment, bringing guests to club meetings so they can see the benefits of Toastmasters membership, and maintaining honest and ethical standards during the conduct of all Toastmasters activities.

For club leaders, integrity also means focusing on members' needs and achievements in our program.

What does **respect** mean in our clubs? For club members respect means understanding that each member is unique, possessing certain skills and abilities, goals and ambitions, and strengths and weaknesses. For club leaders it also means understanding that each member is developing at his or her own pace, and while some may need a gentle push from time to time, others need space to develop.

What does **service** mean in our clubs? For club members service means stepping up when required to help the club function as a stellar learning environment for the benefit of all members. For club leaders service also means focusing on the planning and delivery of an environment and a varied program conducive to member achievement.

What does **excellence** mean in our clubs? For club members excellence means performing assigned duties to the best of our ability every time. Sometimes we have bad days, and sometimes we have less time to prepare than we might like. Regardless, excellence means performing to the best of our ability every time for the benefit of the club and all the members. For club leaders, excellence relates directly to our organization's strategic plan and to providing an atmosphere of club excellence that enables member achievement.

Values drive culture. Values drive action. Our Toastmasters core values enable club excellence and member achievement. I hope all of our clubs take the opportunity to discuss our core values during a round of Table Topics.

July 2016 Intention

In this column I chose to write about change, the challenges of change, and the need for an organization to evolve. Prior to 2016 our policies required that all club meetings were to be held in a face-to-face environment only. Our policy was not congruent with the changes video capabilities enabled. We were aware that there were some clubs deviating from this policy. The business world certainly embraced video conferencing. The board recognized the need to support online meetings as often business meetings were held on video, so we changed the policy to support online meetings.

There was some resistance in the organization. Some believed the face-to-face environment was superior to online. Some believed that the imminent, revised educational platform with material residing primarily online, might leave more senior members behind, even though a print option was available.

Change is difficult in organizations. Technological change can be particularly disruptive. However, organizations need to adapt as the broader environment evolves. The environment was moving to more online service delivery and engagement. And of course, unknown at the time, 2020 would see the COVID-19 pandemic hugely reduce face-to-face contact.

So, I wrote a column about how technology affected a participant in the tourism business and related their challenges to Toastmasters.

July 2016 Viewpoint

Face to Face Communication

Recently I was reading an article in a local newspaper about a beautiful tourist bureau located in a refurbished, covered bridge here in New Brunswick, Canada. In recent years, tourists kept stopping in to use the restrooms but left without picking up maps or brochures, or without asking the volunteer staff about local attractions. That's because tourists these days plan their itineraries online and then rely on the GPS unit in their car or phone for directions. The business of tourism has changed. And the beautiful tourist bureau is now available for purchase. I have to wonder if it could have evolved in some way to remain more relevant to travelers.

Business changes quickly these days. I've been asked if Toastmasters is still relevant in our increasingly digital world. Of course we are! More than ever. Toastmasters exists to empower people to become more effective communicators and leaders. And club meetings are the vehicle for letting members practice these vital soft skills.

Toastmasters now allows online clubs, providing an additional opportunity for members to practice communication skills in virtual environments. Every day many of our members participate in teleconferences and video conferences in their professional lives. I've personally participated in Cisco TelePresence video conferences so realistic-looking that people have banged a hand on a wall trying to pass a pen to a virtual counterpart.

Online clubs complement our face-to-face meetings. Our Board of Directors approved the existence of such clubs because Toastmasters has a role in enabling effective communication in online environments. However, I do believe that many new members who are attracted to our online clubs will also see the value of participating in our in-person clubs. Face to face is the essence of human communication, still more personal than online environments.

In his book <u>Contagious: Why Things Catch On</u>, Jonah Berger challenges readers to consider what percentage of word-of-mouth communication happens online—through tweets, emails, blog posts, etc. —versus face to face. He indicates that only seven percent of it happens online. We tend to overestimate this dynamic because it's easy to see tweets, emails and posts. It's much harder to measure conversation. But conversation and face to face still dominate.

Toastmasters has made great gains with technology in our very personal business. At Toastmasters World Headquarters, new member applications, education awards and member payments are all entered online. Members order from online catalogs and rarely from print catalogs. Not long ago that was not the norm.

Toastmasters has adopted many new technologies. Our services and environment must be relevant to the way members live and work. However, our face-to-face club meetings will remain relevant and at the core of the Toastmasters experience for many years to come.

August 2016 Strategy

In April, I completed and submitted my final column for publication in the August issue. This was the lead time required for preparation of the magazine. The August column provided an opportunity to write about the annual changeover in our club leadership positions, in my position of International President, among many others in the organization.

I wanted to make clear my commitment to remain a member. My membership in Toastmasters has shaped me, and continues to do so. The opportunity to regularly exercise communication and soft skills, and receive feedback on my performance is immensely valuable.

Another element to transitions sees past leaders supporting successor leaders, and gracefully getting out of the way of the successors. I've observed some people struggle with stepping to the background, and instead only offering a quiet word with successors when appropriate.

Managing transitions is a component of leadership. This column was intended to encourage current leaders to support an orderly transition, and support the new leadership teams as they stepped into their positions.

August 2016 Viewpoint

100,000 Volunteer Leaders

From 2015-2016 and now onto 2016-2017. A time of transition in Toastmasters. Each year we have over

100,000 volunteer leaders in our clubs and in the organization. Many now leave leadership positions in Toastmasters, and many take on new positions. Including me.

At the conclusion of our convention in Washington I take on the role of Immediate Past International President, and a year later in Vancouver I will leave the Toastmasters board. I'm conscious of this as a current leader and soon-to-be past leader. Many of you face similar transitions.

I have been a Toastmaster continuously since 1987. At times I've been heavily involved and at times less involved. This is because I always look for the best opportunity to contribute and at the same time to advance my skills. Sometimes that's in Toastmasters. But sometimes my best opportunity has been in a work environment or in a volunteer role with another organization.

I hope you've noticed that we've begun sharing stories in The Toastmaster magazine about past members who have used skills we've enabled to advance other causes. Jimmy Thai in Vietnam. Speaker of the House in Canada Geoff Reagan, MP. I hope you take pride in the role Toastmasters has played in enabling these individuals to contribute to our broader world and society, and I hope you see much opportunity personally and for the members in your club.

In Washington, D.C., Mike Storkey steps into the role of International President. He's ready for this volunteer job. I have struggled at times with transitions like this one. But this is part of the role of a volunteer leader. I'm eager to support Mike and all of our new leadership teams as they begin their work in continuing to serve our clubs and members. I expect from time to time I'll be asked for my views and from time to time I'll offer an observation or opinion for consideration. I trust our new teams to commit to our mission and deliver for our members and clubs. I'm confident our club leaders will continue to provide excellent environments which will enable their members to achieve amazing results inside and outside of Toastmasters.

Author Annie Dillard wrote;

"How we spend our days is, of course, how we spend our lives."

Consistent with this I will always be a Toastmaster. I want to keep my communication and leadership skills sharp. And to be strong as a leader or speaker we need a base of knowledge, a place to practice these skills, and feedback on our performance. I can't think of another place where these three elements are better enabled for individuals who desire to practice and improve their skills.

It has been my pleasure to serve as International President. I look forward to seeing many of you at convention in Washington and celebrating your achievements.

Conclusion

I wrote this book for people who are stepping into new leadership positions and have opportunity to communicate with their teams with written material, among other methods. I had opportunity to communicate broadly with a monthly column. I've shared the strategy behind each of those columns. Preparing a list of potential topics in advance helped me immensely in clarifying my view of how the organization could evolve.

The clarity enabled by my list of potential topics, and my writing on these topics improved my speaking, as well as my writing. As you prepare for your new role, I encourage you to jot down any ideas you have in a phone or notepad. I usually have one or more 5x7 notepads nearby and continue to record speech ideas, blog content ideas, and book concepts. If you'd like to visit my Grow Your Comfort Zone blog please visit https://gycz.blogspot.com/

If you're interested in my other books please visit amazon.com/author/jimkokocki

Best wishes.

Appendix A – Initial Email to Staff Outlining Topics

I've drafted a list of potential Viewpoint topics. My September Viewpoint is on driving awareness and knowledge with pictures from club meetings. I won't, and can't, use all of these, and will add others as the year progresses. But I'll share them so you can see what messaging I believe is important.

1. Likely one on situational leadership from Blanchard and Hersey. One of the key points is when people are assigned a new task, they have low "task maturity" and must be told what to do – in a professional manner. That's not demeaning, it's respectful of someone's development.

2. Maybe something else on public relations and driving awareness and knowledge to build our funnel of potential members

3. Something about "alumni.'" I know we've had members join a club and participate for six months, get what they needed, and went on to do amazing things in their communities and businesses. They'll still say good things about Toastmasters although

they bring our average length stats down. This theme is about keeping some sort of connection and perhaps recognition.

4. Avoiding trying to motivate people by email – I believe people rely on it far too much

5. Member's pride in their clubs and the strength of our worldwide network of clubs. If WHQ was out of commission for a month, our clubs would still serve our members very well.

6. Maybe something on positional power and personal power

7. Something on waiting too long to develop leadership skills and Toastmasters position in regard to this. This relates to a blog by Jack Zenger in HBR where he writes about protecting the self-esteem of colleagues and focusing on problems and not personalities.

8. Selecting and working with a mentor and how our needs from mentors change as we evolve.

9. Leading virtual teams

10. Getting the right prospective member to the right club, e.g. getting a professional woman to the highly professional local club, and the blue collar guy to a more casual club if that's what he needs.

11. Adapting to audiences and culturally relevant behaviors. I'm interested in this from the perspective of corporate visits and foreign countries.

12. Self-evaluation and assessment of leadership skills and behaviors.